MARRYING ACCIDENTALLY
the story of Hatsuko Takara

MARRYING ACCIDENTALLY

the story of Hatsuko Takara

Amos Malupenga

NISC

Published in South Africa on behalf of the author
by NISC (Pty) Ltd, PO Box 377, Makhanda, 6140, South Africa
www.nisc.co.za

First edition, first impression 2024
© Amos Malupenga 2024
email: conversationsmalupenga@gmail.com

ISBN: 978-1-920033-16-3 (softcover)

Design and layout: NISC (Pty) Ltd
Editing: Jack Zimba
Proofreading: Peter Lague
Cover design: Sakabilo Kalembwe, concept by Amos Malupenga
Cover photograph: Evans Mwila

All photographs, unless stated otherwise, are from Hatsuko Takara's family album.

D E D I C A T I O N

First
To all visually impaired people in Zambia
and the world over.

Second
To the teachers who have taken up special education
to impart knowledge and skills to learners
who are differently abled.

CONTENTS

PROLOGUE

A Business Card

✳✳✳

IT was a Friday afternoon, September 23, 2022, in the Kenneth Kaunda Hall at the Mulungushi International Conference Centre in Lusaka. I found myself among scores of people that had paid to attend a lecture on entrepreneurship organised by Eden University.

I seldom – if ever at all – attend such lectures, but this time I was compelled to because the event had been extensively advertised, highlighting the main speaker.

Professor Patrick Loch Otieno Lumumba, that eloquent Kenyan legal luminary fondly known as Prof. PLO, was listed as the keynote speaker. I enjoy listening to his usually unscripted thought-provoking presentations which are often widely shared on various social media platforms. Therefore, the opportunity for me to listen to him in person was irresistible.

But before him, a number of speakers made their presentations, with Kelvin Kaunda, the founder of Eden University, giving a testimony of how he had conceived the idea of setting up a university, and how he has lived to witness its phenomenal growth.

Then came Prof. Lumumba's turn to deliver his much-awaited talk. He is renowned for speaking his mind, an attribute that sometimes brushes some government leaders on the African continent the wrong way.

I still recall, how a few years before this event, the professor had been denied entry into Zambia, forced back to his country moments after he landed at Kenneth Kaunda International Airport in Lusaka. He had been invited to make a presentation at a similar event organised by the same university.

The reasons for refusing him entry, as far as I can remember, were vague and baseless. This was because the government could not really find proper reasons for barring Prof. Lumumba. Most people, broadly and justifiably so, speculated that his previous caustic criticism of the government of Zambia on governance issues meant that he had become persona non grata with the regime at the time.

It was against that backdrop that Prof. Lumumba was addressing this highly expectant gathering in Lusaka. During such presentations, dissension and Prof. Lumumba are often inseparable. So he started by subtly 'dissing' the speakers before him, who – in his implied opinion – assumed that everyone in the audience understood what entrepreneurship was and, therefore, never cared to define the term. It was those types of presentations, Prof. Lumumba said, that made such meetings ineffective.

And so in trying to get his audience to understand and appreciate what entrepreneurship was, Prof. Lumumba asked a few rhetorical questions which I still recall, albeit not word for word.

"Isn't an entrepreneur that person, who – using their skills and sometimes initiative – seizes an opportunity or opportunities to start or own a business for a livelihood and finds success and makes profits by taking risks?" he asked the eager audience that gave him their undivided attention. "Isn't an entrepreneur that individual who, against all odds, starts a new business amidst such risks but enjoys most of the rewards, the profit?" he continued.

The professor then proceeded to develop his presentation which was, at regular intervals, disrupted by applause from the audience, culminating in a standing ovation at his conclusion. It was an afternoon of intense motivation providing a number of take-home points. Two, however, stood out for me.

First: "You can't teach people experience. Let them experience *experience* if they have to learn experience."

Second: "The bigger the dream, the better the opportunity. So go and dream but wake up to live that dream. Don't oversleep or fail to wake up!"

Apart from the professor, one other speaker who stood out for me was Chibamba Kanyama, a Zambian journalist of long standing, who is also an economist, communications expert and diplomat.

He, too, had a lot to share. Among others, was a lesson about the importance of a *business card* which, of course, at the time sounded rather mundane.

"A business card is very important," he said. "Don't throw away a business card because you may need it in future, keep it safe. It can be very useful and result in business you never ever imagined getting."

To drive the point home, Chibamba shared an anecdote about an incident that occurred when he was working for the Zambia State Insurance Corporation.

He said he had once given his business card to a lady who, during the course of their conversation, rolled it up and used it as cotton bud to clean her ear. She definitely must have thrown it away afterwards.

"I was so offended and angry, but restrained myself," Chibamba recalled, "because I knew that the chance of any future business with that lady was no doubt lost."

I didn't take the lesson on the business card very seriously, but casually filed it in my memory. I would only appreciate it four months later.

As the year 2023 began, I resolved to keep my records at home tidier and discard documents that had outlived their usefulness. That was on January 10. During this process, I pulled out an old office bag that I had used many years ago when I worked as a journalist at *The*

Post newspaper. I had completely forgotten about this bag. I didn't even realise that it was stashed somewhere in my bedroom. There were various documents in the bag, all of them relating to the time of my thriving career.

Meticulously, I sifted through the bag to ascertain the relevance of the contents. None of the documents passed the test, but I resolved to keep the bag and its contents anyway, purely for sentimental reasons.

As I was about to put away the bag, I checked one last envelope containing business cards and other small items. The cards reminded me of the various people I had met and interacted with as a journalist. Some had grown older and died while others were still alive. Several others had changed jobs and professions, just as I had.

Then my eyes fell upon one business card bearing the name: *H. Takara-Kalabula (Mrs),* with two mobile numbers scribbled in ink and a home number printed on it.

In 2006 I first met Mrs Hatsuko Takara-Kalabula, a Japanese woman who had lived in Zambia since 1977. On a visit in 2007, she gave me her business card. Her husband, Dr Mwamba Darlington Kalabula, who was a University of Zambia lecturer, sadly died in 2008 and when I went to pay my respects to his widow at the family residence in Kalundu, in Lusaka, I found that Mrs Hatsuko Takara-Kalabula had relocated. I had lost contact with her.

I was very keen to renew our acquaintance but was now apparently stuck and lost because I could not find the business card she had given me and had not transferred the details to my phone's contact list. I knew I had the card somewhere, but could not tell exactly where. It was only 16 years later that I found it, when sorting through the contents of my office bag.

There and then, I phoned Mrs Hatsuko Takara-Kalabula and was delighted to hear her voice on the other end of the line. She, too, was enchanted to hear mine.

We talked and laughed over the phone for a long time, reminiscing about the past. As we concluded the conversation, she invited me over to her new home. "My dear, I am now 90 years old," she said cheerfully, although she had just celebrated her 89th birthday on December 12, 2022. "Come we discuss. You and I have to do something big this year."

It was during my visit to Mrs Takara-Kalabula's home that this book project was conceived.

"I have been thinking about you, looking for you all this time ... you are the only one I could think of to write my simple life-story in a simple way," she said heartily.

Coincidentally, and unbeknown to me, Mrs Takara-Kalabula had also been looking for my phone number over the years as she sought to reconnect with me, having lost or misplaced my business card. A few days prior to my contacting her, she had – in fact – requested Mr Sunday Musonda, who worked as a Special Assistant in the office of the late Dr Kenneth Kaunda, Zambia's founding president, to help find my phone number and pass it on to her. And when I phoned her, she was so certain Mr Musonda's efforts had finally yielded something.

"Did Mr Musonda pass on my message to you? I have been looking for you like a needle in a haystack," she said.

In that moment, I remembered Chibamba Kanyama's counsel: "A business card is very important. Don't throw away a business card because you may need it in future, keep it safe. It can be very useful and result in business you never ever imagined getting."

******

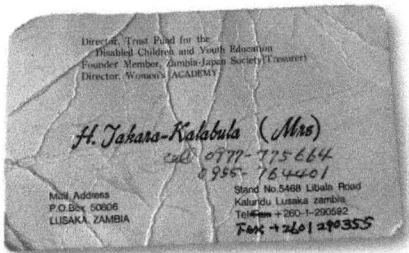

HATSUKO in her first year at Ryukyu University in Okinawa, 1952.

CHAPTER ONE

Hatsuko – The Beginning

✳✳✳

I T was December 12, 1933 on the small, quiet, peaceful island of Okinawa in Japan when a baby girl was born to begin a long journey into the unforeseen and unknown future. The baby was named Hatsuko Takara. 'Hatsuko' in Japanese means 'first born daughter' or the 'beginning', which was very apt, for the baby was the first child of Chugen and Kiyoko Takara.

Many years later, Hatsuko would venture into Africa, Zambia in particular, notwithstanding the frightening picture of the continent the Europeans she had contact with during her sojourn in Britain painted for her, of a place roaming with dangerous wild animals like lions and elephants, and plagued by disease.

In July 1977, Hatsuko flew to Zambia aboard a British Airways flight and landed at Lusaka International Airport (now Kenneth Kaunda International Airport).

In no time, she 'fell in love' with pupils at a school for the blind in the City of Ndola, largely because of the challenges and difficulties they faced. And before long, she found herself in a romantic relationship with the school's headmaster, Mwamba Darlington Kalabula, the man who, as a platonic friend, had actually invited her to Zambia.

This relationship resulted in marriage the following year. That is how Hatsuko Takara became Hatsuko Takara-Kalabula and made Zambia her second home.

***

Hatsuko was born into an affluent family that lived on a large estate on Okinawa Island, in the southern part of Japan. Her only sibling, Chusei, was born in 1937, two years before the outbreak of the Second World War. He would later train to become a veterinary surgeon.

Hatsuko's father – Chugen – was a prosperous businessman who owned properties. In the early 1940s, after the beginning of the Second World War, Chugen moved to Manila, in the Philippines, where he had earlier established businesses. And that was the last his family saw of him. Later they would learn that Chugen had been conscripted into the Japanese army to fight against the invading Americans.

Before the war, Chugen had spent considerable time in Manila doing business and had learnt to speak the local language. Because of his proficiency in the Filipino language, Chugen was sent to the battlefront, on the border between Japan and the Philippines. Unfortunately, he was among the many Japanese who lost their lives as the war intensified.

According to records, as many as two-thirds of the Japanese troops died in 1943 after suffering from illness and starvation due to a shortage of supplies, especially food, medicines, munitions, and armaments. This was largely occasioned by the United States of America (USA) submarine interdiction of supplies and losses to Japanese shipping, which was worsened by a longstanding rivalry with the Imperial Japanese Navy. Consequently, large numbers of fighter aircraft became unserviceable for lack of spare parts.

Chugen's family was not aware of the circumstances surrounding his death; they could only speculate that either he died of starvation or illness, or was shot by the invading enemy.

"I was very young then," recalls Hatsuko. "Our family was later informed about the death of my father. So I didn't enjoy the opportunity to grow up with him. But I generally enjoyed a peaceful childhood in Okinawa brought up by a wonderful grandmother. I think I was a spoiled child."

Before the war broke out in September 1939, Hatsuko remembers being asked, together with other children, to take bamboo sticks to school to use as 'guns' against the American soldiers. As a little girl, she didn't understand the logic in that act, and even in her old age, she still wonders why she and the other children were asked to play 'shooting' with bamboo sticks.

"We didn't even know that some atomic bombs were being developed," she says. "When the war started, there was a lot of scampering and no food. Japanese soldiers even used our estate on the island as a hiding place. We were later told to vacate the island for the mainland. And we did just that using a ship. We returned to the island after the war."

But they returned to an island that now lay ruinous, heavily scarred by the war.

Hatsuko remembers being marched with her fellow pupils out of class to go and clear human remains that littered Okinawa.

"We were in primary school then, grade five, if I remember correctly. So we would learn up to the end of the morning and in the afternoon go to collect human skeletons of the people who had died in the war as a way of clearing the land," recalls Hatsuko.

"The bones were put in sacks. We also collected cartridges. These sacks of bones were heaped in the field near our school. After that they were taken somewhere, where a monument was erected."

Due to the destruction resulting from the war, Japan had to be rebuilt. Part of the Takara estate was surrendered to the state and used to build a school.

Hatsuko spent six years in primary school, three in junior secondary and another three in senior secondary. She completed high school in 1952 and set her sights on going to university. But there was an English Teachers' Training College established after the war so that the Japanese could learn how to speak English. Having defeated Japan, the allies were led by the USA in the occupation and rehabilitation of the Japanese state between 1945 and 1952. The occupying USA forces enacted widespread military, political, economic, and social reforms.

"So, from high school, we went to this English college. After this, we proceeded to university. But learning did not start immediately," says Hatsuko.

"We first had to help in the construction of the university. By the time the university was ready to operate, my mother fell ill, so I couldn't proceed with my university education. I had to quit in order take care of my sick mother and younger brother, Chusei. My brother later finished high school and was admitted to university in Tokyo to study veterinary medicine."

It was only after Chusei was settled in the School of Veterinary Medicine that Hatsuko found a job with American Express, in the banking section. She did not stay there for long; she resigned and found a job as a receptionist for a newspaper called *Morning Star.*

"I used to get a lot of money," says Hatsuko with nostalgia.

As is usually the case in most economies worldwide, government or quasi government institutions and parastatal companies are deemed to offer better employment security. For this reason, Kiyoko, Takara's mother, persuaded her daughter to join a parastatal company dealing in oil.

But there was a challenge in that this oil company mainly employed men, particularly as tank drivers. Therefore, job opportunities for women were rare. Luckily and as a pleasant surprise for Hatsuko, an opportunity for secretarial services arose in the company managing director's office.

"I served the company's managing director for two-and-half years," she reminisces. "After that, I decided to go back to school. It was an institution attached to Hawaii, an American school so I could go back to Okinawa. Okinawa was now being governed by the Americans after they had defeated Japan. So we had to learn the American way of life, especially in education. We had a lot of relatives in Hawaii from Okinawa. Later, in the early 1970s, we heard that Okinawa was going back to Japan. So, I decided to return to my home, which was in Tokyo, from Hawaii."

In Tokyo, Hatsuko found employment with an American publishing company.

"I had the opportunity to study without buying books," she recalls.

Not far from where Hatsuko worked was the British Embassy, which she visited frequently, and eventually developed an interest in studying in Britain.

"I applied to study in Britain because a lot of people in Okinawa were getting scholarships to study in America. So, I saved money to study in Britain because now I was looking after myself. I developed an interest in reading a lot of books. Most of my friends [who survived the Second World War] were married by this time. But, because I was not married, I just developed a good friendship with books."

In 1971, Hatsuko was admitted to Aoyama-Gakuin University in Tokyo to pursue a Bachelor of Arts in English/American Literature. She graduated in 1975 and decided to undertake a postgraduate programme in the United Kingdom.

"Because the Japanese had difficulties pronouncing some English words or pronouncing them in a British way, I chose to go to England to study linguistics, especially phonetics,[1] so that I could teach my fellow people the correct pronunciation of English," says Hatsuko.

****

---

1 *Phonetics is a branch of linguistics that studies how humans produce and perceive sounds, or in the case of sign language, the equivalent aspects of sign. Linguists who specialise in studying the physical properties of speech are called phoneticians.*

TOP: Hatsuko, seated in the front row between Mwamba Darlington Kalabula (on her left) and his good friend Abel Lukulu Bwalya (on her right) in Edinburgh during a get-together function as international students, 1977.

BOTTOM: Abel Lukulu Bwalya (left) and Mwamba Darlington Kalabula in Lusaka long after their return from Edinburgh.

CHAPTER TWO

Manchester and Edinburgh

✳✳✳

ETERMINED to advance her academic qualifications, Hatsuko arrived at Manchester University in Britain in 1975 to embark on a postgraduate programme in *linguistics*, the scientific study of language and its structure, including the study of grammar, syntax, and phonetics. But it was phonetics that Hatsuko was most interested in because she really wanted to help her fellow countrymen and women with the pronunciation of English when she returned to Japan.

The following year, in her quest to acquire skills in teaching English to Japanese people as a foreign language, Hatsuko enrolled with the Moray House School of Education, a school within the College of Arts, Humanities and Social Science at the University of Edinburgh in Scotland. She enrolled to pursue a Diploma in TESOL (Teaching English to Speakers of Other Languages).

Here Hatsuko met two young Zambian men, Abel Bwalya and Mwamba Darlington Kalabula, both pursuing further studies in special education. Bwalya was a teacher for the deaf, while Kalabula taught visually-impaired students. Displaying no assumptions of inclinations towards a romantic relationship while they were in Edinburgh, Kalabula would, two years later, become Hatsuko's husband.

Kalabula had been born into a very humble family in Chief Nkolemfumu's area in the Kasama District in northern Zambia in 1946. He went to Mulobola Mission School up to Standard Four. When he was selected to progress to Standard Five, he could not because his family was too poor to afford his school fees. So, he moved to Ndola where he joined his uncle and continued with his education. There, in 1962, he enrolled in Form One at Masala Secondary School. Shortly thereafter, he moved to Livingstone where he did Form Two. Because of his family's continued financial challenges, Kalabula had to return to Ndola which, with the thriving mining industry, offered better financial prospects. Unfortunately, these prospects never materialised for Kalabula, and he was unable to complete his Grade 12, or Form Five, as it was then called.

Luckily, in those days, entry to tertiary institutions was not as competitive as is the case today. With his humble junior secondary school qualifications, Kalabula was able to enrol for a teaching programme at Mufulira Teachers' Training College in 1966.

Upon completion of his teaching course, in 1967, he worked as a teacher in Chingola.

In 1973, Kalabula, who had developed great interest in teaching differently-abled children, travelled to Lusaka to train as a teacher for the disabled at Lusaka College for Teachers of the Handicapped. He was trained to teach children with visual impairments. In the meantime, he had continued his secondary school education and in due course passed six subjects at O'level (ordinary level). In later years, this would enable him to enrol as a mature student at the University of Zambia to study via distance learning.

After this training in Lusaka, Kalabula was posted to Lions School for the Blind in Ndola. It was a newly established school and Kalabula was its first headmaster, with only five pupils. He worked so hard that he built up the numbers from five to sixty.

In 1976, while growing the pupil numbers at Lions School, Kalabula was awarded a Commonwealth scholarship to study in Edinburgh, Scotland. The area of study at diploma level was in teaching children with special needs. It was here that Kalabula met Hatsuko, as a fellow foreign student. A platonic relationship ensued, arising from Hatsuko's interest in getting to know Kalabula better, particularly about his work as a teacher for the blind, coupled with her desire to introduce him to Buddhism. One day, she invited him to a Buddhist meeting in Glasgow where he found himself the only black person among the many white faces.

"I found this awkward," Kalabula said in an interview in 2007. "I was the only differently coloured person there, but the respect and the way they treated me was amazing, having come from the colonial period where each person had a place."

Hatsuko had her own recollections about what drew her close to the two Zambian teachers, in particular Kalabula.

"These two were always talking about the future of Zambia. They were very passionate about it. This was during Dr Kenneth Kaunda's era of the UNIP government," she recalls. "I was very impressed about it. They were very futuristic in their thinking."

She also noticed that because of the limited nature of their scholarships, the two Zambian students had to engage in plenty of cost-saving measures. "They were even cooking for themselves," Hatsuko remembers. "I sympathised with them."

But she loved and enjoyed listening to Bwalya and Kalabula when they spoke English because she was interested in how they pronounced words.

"I think it was destiny because if I hadn't gone to Scotland from Manchester University, I would not have met these two gentlemen," she said.

Because Bwalya and Kalabula were rather large in comparison to Japanese people, Hatsuko assumed the two gentlemen were in their 50s. Kalabula was in fact 13 years younger than Hatsuko.

"They were huge but soft-spoken, nice gentlemen. I was small," she says, as she remembers how she was fascinated by Kalabula's long and thick hair, which she would innocently touch from time to time. "I thought they could protect me from anything."

Typically, on Saturdays, Hatsuko would go to a Chinese restaurant for a meal. But after befriending Bwalya and Kalabula, she once invited them to accompany her to the restaurant because it was often boring to eat out alone. They enjoyed this occasion so much that it turned into a regular Saturday outing.

Before long, the students were graduating with diplomas and had to go their separate ways. Hatsuko graduated with a postgraduate Diploma in TESOL. Kalabula obtained a diploma in teaching children with special needs.

Because of the bond of friendship that now existed among the three friends – the two Zambian men and the petite Japanese lady – the end of the university programme could not end their friendship. In fact, their graduation provided an opportunity for Hatsuko to step onto a trajectory of a life-long partnership and friendship with Kalabula and Bwalya.

"As we were leaving Edinburgh, the two gentlemen invited me to visit Zambia and see its beauty, if chance allowed," Hatsuko recalls nostalgically.

****

Coming to Zambia

✳✳✳

THE invitation to visit Zambia was as tempting as it was frightening for Hatsuko. On the one hand, she was excited at the prospect of visiting Africa, especially Zambia, for the first time. Not even in her wildest dreams had she ever dreamt of one day travelling to Africa. She tried to imagine what would happen upon her arrival in the 'jungle' should she choose to accept Bwalya and Kalabula's invitation. Many Europeans back then associated Africa with wild animals and all manner of backwardness and had painted a picture of a terrifying place for Hatsuko, so all she could imagine were dangerous wild animals, which scared her.

On the other hand, Hatsuko entertained the thought of returning to Manchester University to pursue a master's degree programme. But she was drawn by her own curiosity to see what sort of place Zambia was and so the desire to visit the country grew stronger. She finally decided she would not allow her fear to stop her from travelling and that she would travel to Zambia against all odds.

Ironically, Hatsuko would later, in 2008, graduate with a master's degree from the University of Zambia, and not Manchester University.

Having resolved to honour the invitation from the two Zambian friends whom, in jest, she sometimes referred to as young elephants, Hatsuko went to the Zambian Mission in London to apply for a visa.

"I was warmly received. I asked what procedures I needed to follow in order to visit my friends in Lusaka," Hatsuko remembers. "They gave me some forms to complete and indicated that they would give me a short-term visa. On the visa application form, I was required to state my race but this confused me. I didn't know how to answer that because I only knew of one race on earth, the human race. So I told them I would write 'human race' in that space. The officers laughed, they enjoyed that. They asked me to come back after lunch and when I did, I found the visa ready for collection. I went straight to a travel agent and bought an air ticket for a British Airways flight to Lusaka. This was in July 1977. By this time, Mr Kalabula was heading a newly established school for the blind in Ndola, while Mr Bwalya was teaching at a mission school. So we agreed that I would communicate with Mr Bwalya through Mr. Kalabula."

After several hours aboard the British Airways flight, Hatsuko set foot on Zambian soil for the very first time. It was a whole new world for her as she eagerly looked in vain for the much expected wild animals. What she did see, however, were what she called the 'improper' road(s) leading her to Lusaka Hotel in the Central Business District where she was booked to lodge for a night before proceeding to Ndola the following day. It was a restful night for Hatsuko amidst that unique hospitality for which Zambia is renowned.

In those days, the main inter-city road transport was serviced by a parastatal company, the United Bus Company of Zambia (UBZ). So Hatsuko boarded a UBZ bus from Lusaka to Ndola, a stretch of slightly over 300 kilometres.

"I was surprised to see that the bus engine was actually inside, somewhere behind, in the back and just covered," she recalled in an apparent reference to today's phenomenal development in this sector. "It was a *sunka mulamu* [a vehicle that is not in very good

HATSUKO, attired in a traditional African Chitenge dress to publicise Zambia in particular and Africa in general during her visit to Okinawa in the early 1980s.

condition, hence not so reliable]. You can imagine the noise, the heat and some smoke [escaping, filtering through the passenger space]."

That notwithstanding, Hatsuko enjoyed the bus ride as she anticipated seeing some wild animals along the way.

"I was surprised that all the way from Lusaka to Ndola, I didn't see any animals and yet I was told that if I travelled to Africa, or Zambia, in particular, I would be devoured by animals like lions," she said. "People would get onto the bus and drop off at regular intervals; so many stop-overs! They would even squeeze themselves on a seat. They also drank Coca-Cola and Fanta on the bus. This was unexpected."

******

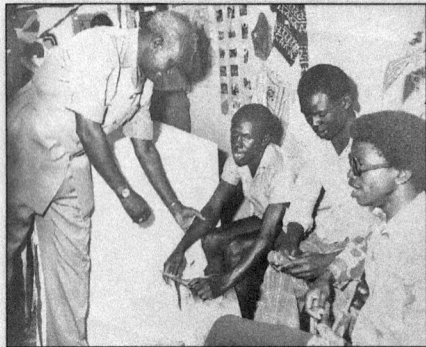

Presented by
JAPAN WORLD EXPOSITION
COMMEMORATIVE ASSOCIATION

CHAPTER FOUR

'In Love with the Blind'

✳✳✳

After a few hours on the road, the UBZ *sunka mulamu* arrived in Ndola. Hatsuko was to lodge, for a number of days, at Savoy Hotel, an upmarket hotel at the time. She was happy to reconnect with Kalabula, her friend, in his homeland. Her initial plan was to visit for no longer than two weeks. But the plan changed after she interacted with the blind pupils and became familiar with their challenges.

In the mid to late 1970s, Zambia – under the leadership of its founding president Dr Kenneth Kaunda – was leading the frontline states that played a pivotal role in the liberation struggle for Southern Rhodesia (now Zimbabwe) and southern Africa in general. This did

TOP: (left) Hatsuko and headmaster Mwamba Kalabula posing for a photograph with some blind pupils from a music class at Ndola School for the Blind, 1978; (right) Hatsuko in Okinawa shortly after giving a media interview about Zambia, 1979.

MIDDLE: (upper left) President Kenneth Kaunda interacting with some blind pupils at the International Trade Fair in Ndola, 1978; (right) Hatsuko shaking hands with then President of Zambia, Dr Kenneth Kaunda, when he visited the stand at the International Trade Fair in Ndola where the school for the blind had exhibited. Behind her is headmaster Mwamba Kalabula, 1978; (lower left) Hatsuko, handing over the public address system (a donation from well-wishers in Japan) to the Ndola School for the Blind through the then district Chief Education Officer. Looking on is headmaster Mwamba Kalabula, 1978..

BOTTOM: Pupils enjoying the services of a minibus donated to the school by the Japan World Exposition Commemorative Association through Hatsuko's facilitation to mitigate the school's transport challenges.

not happen without any adverse effects on the country's economy. The consequences of retaliation by the apartheid regime in South Africa, besides Zambia's own sacrifices of financial, material, human and other resources, affected the country's economic development and growth. Zambia experienced an economic meltdown.

Shortages of food and other essential commodities were not uncommon. The Ndola School for the Blind, as it was called then (now Ndola Lions School for the Visually Impaired), was not spared in this regard. The school resorted to cultivating maize and sweet potatoes, using part of its land, to supplement the pupils' feeding programme.

It was this situation that engulfed Hatsuko as she spent time with Kalabula at the school.

"I spent time helping Mr Kalabula at the school because he had no female teachers. He only had four teachers; two were blind while the other two were sighted," she says. "But they needed to do a lot of things for the welfare of the blind pupils. Therefore, I extended my stay from two weeks to two months."

Moved with pity, Hatsuko resolved to travel to Japan in September 1977 to mobilise financial and material resources for the school, "due to the challenges I saw there," as she put it.

"I was touched by the suffering that the pupils encountered, including my own experiences, so I went back to Japan to mobilise in order to help the school in a small way," she says, tracing the genesis of her 'falling in love with the blind pupils'.

First, she had to lobby organisations in Japan to donate a public address system to overcome the communication problems at the school due to the buildings being far apart. The dormitories for female and male pupils were far apart as well as far from the classrooms, dining hall and school compound. The public address system would thus be handy to announce meal times, waking up and lights-out times, as well as to call pupils to assemble whenever the school had visitors. Simply, the public address system would ease general communication within the boarding school community.

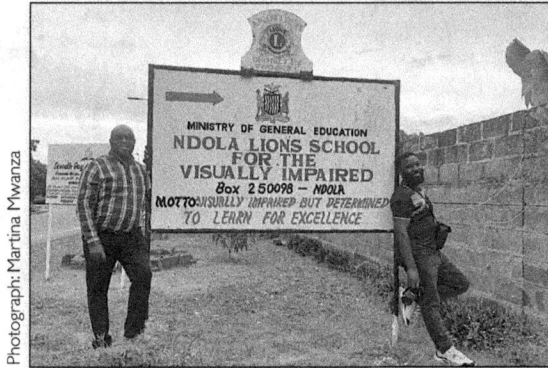

THE AUTHOR (left) with videographer and film maker, Evans Mwila, posing at the signpost for the Ndola Lions School for the Visually Impaired when the duo visited the school, February 2023.

In addition, Hatsuko received donations of electric guitars, which were very rare in Zambia back then, for the pupils' music lessons, and bales of second-hand clothes, bedding and towels for the pupils.

"I also got some financial donations for the school because the monthly budgetary allocation (just over 800 Kwacha, about US$30 at the time of writing) was not enough to feed the pupils and take care of other expenses," she says. "The pupils mostly ate vegetables, beans and *kapenta* [sardines]. So, I started supporting the school by adding to the monthly allocation."

With this going on, Hatsuko started to reconsider her short-term visit to Zambia. Clearly, she was getting personal satisfaction from helping the school and the blind pupils overcome some of their challenges. She soon had no more debate within herself whether to leave or stay; she came to the conclusion that should extend her stay for a longer or even indefinite period.

Hatsuko then decided to postpone her return indefinitely, to either Manchester in the United Kingdom or Tokyo in Japan.

"I decided to stay in Zambia a little longer and help Mr Kalabula to manage the school because I had fallen in love with the blind pupils," says Hatsuko.

❉

TOP: (left) Hatsuko and Kalabula had two separate wedding ceremonies, one in Zambia and the other in Japan. Here, Hatsuko is posing during the ceremony in Okinawa, Japan, 1981; (right) Hatsuko and Kalabula cutting the cake during their wedding ceremony in Ndola, 1978.

MIDDLE: Kalabula, arriving at the airport in Japan on his first visit to Okinawa, 1981.

BOTTOM: (left) Hatsuko and Kalabula enjoying the beach in Okinawa, 1981; (centre) Hatsuko and her adopted son, Ipe, during her graduation at the University of Zambia, 2008; (right) Dr Kalabula and Hatsuko in Lusaka, 2007 He had graduated with a PhD in 1992. [Photograph: Thomas Nsama]

CHAPTER FIVE

Marrying 'Accidentally'

✻✳✻

Hatsuko, whose love for the pupils at the school for the blind was daily becoming more deeply ingrained, found Kalabula's passion for and commitment to the school an adorable source of immense inspiration and motivation. She even sought to formalise her association with the school when she applied to become a teacher at the same institution. That was early in 1978.

Regrettably, the Ministry of Education turned down her application for she was considered over-qualified for the job. But perhaps the fact that she did not possess any qualifications in special education was the major obstacle. The authorities advised that Hatsuko could instead be offered an opportunity to teach or lecture in any secondary school or teachers' training college in the Copperbelt Province or Lusaka.

Hatsuko's heart was broken by that response.

"How could I go to teach in Lusaka or any other town when my decision to remain in Zambia was purely based on my desire to assist the school for the blind?" Hatsuko wondered.

Despite the negative feedback from the Ministry of Education, Hatsuko's desire and resolve to work for the school for the blind remained strong. Consequently, she declared herself a 'volunteer staff member' of the school and continued to mobilise resources as she worked closely with Kalabula, who she says was 'a good organiser'.

Because the school did not have enough funding, the diet for the pupils comprised mainly vegetables, beans and *kapenta*. But occasionally, Kalabula would buy some meaty bones so that the pupils could enjoy a rare treat.

Sometime in July 1978, the annual *Umutomboko* traditional ceremony of the Lunda people in Kawambwa District of Luapula Province was scheduled to take place. The ceremony celebrates the conquest of the Lunda in wars with other tribes about three centuries ago. The climax is a conquest dance performed by the chief himself, dressed in a long colourful skirt and headdress.

Kalabula decided to seize the opportunity to introduce Hatsuko to one of Zambia's traditional ceremonies and culture. He also planned to use the opportunity to buy dried fish which was cheaper in that part of the country, which has many rivers and lakes. This would help the school greatly.

At the time, the school received a monthly allocation of 870 Kwacha to feed 56 pupils and pay all its bills, including electricity and water. This was insufficient to meet all the needs of the school. One of Kalabula's initiatives was to find ways to enhance the pupils' diet without spending too much money. He always tried hard to do more with less.

When the time for the trip came, Kalabula packed the school's VW Kombi minibus with his and Hatsuko's bags. They had to drive more than 400 kilometres to get to Kawambwa from Ndola.

For Hatsuko, however, it was the fish buying activity that she really looked forward to and not the traditional ceremony. That's how much she cared about the school and the pupils.

"We were four in the vehicle and Mr Kalabula was the one driving," she recollects. "There was the [official] driver, Mr Mbewe who was the office assistant, the headmaster and myself."

Sadly, the trip ended tragically when the minibus overturned, rolling a few times not very far from the destination, in Mwata Kazembe's chiefdom in Kawambwa.

"We were looking forward to meeting the chief but unfortunately we couldn't because of the accident," Hatsuko recollects with melancholy. "I sustained two fractured ribs while Mr Kalabula was injured on his hand. Two of his fingers on his right hand were fractured. One was later put straight but the other was difficult to correct. The other two passengers in the car escaped unhurt."

Arrangements were made for Mr Kalabula and Hatsuko to be evacuated to Mansa, the provincial capital of Luapula Province, initially, and later back to Ndola.

Hatsuko was in great pain. She was transferred to Ndola Central Hospital where only painkillers were administered to her. And to her disbelief, she was merely advised to sleep in a certain position, before being discharged from the hospital.

Hatsuko was not satisfied with the treatment she received from the hospital, but did not complain, nevertheless. However, she made one stark and revealing observation; she didn't see any indigenous doctor in the entire hospital. She was attended to by a young doctor of Asian origin, an Indian to be specific.

This bothered her so much. From that moment, she resolved to support, in whatever way possible, the Zambian students in the School of Medicine at the University of Zambia (UNZA) just to ensure that more indigenous doctors serviced the country's health facilities.

At independence in October 1964, Zambia did not have a university. The very few university graduates in various disciplines in the country had been trained abroad. UNZA was inaugurated in 1966. Among the first intake of students were some who enrolled in the School of Medicine, which had the primary objective of training medical doctors. The first output of graduates, 23 of them, with full medical qualifications was in 1973. Therefore, going by archival statistics, it can safely be assumed that by 1978, Zambia's population of indigenous medical doctors was not in excess of 100. But by 2018, UNZA was graduating more than 100 medical doctors per year, besides those graduating from the various public and private universities which had come onto the scene in the last decade or so.

Hatsuko's full recovery process took about five months. In the meantime, her family in Japan was unaware that she was in Zambia and had been involved in a road traffic accident. As far as they knew, she was still in the United Kingdom pursuing her postgraduate studies.

"It was, therefore, difficult for me to break the news about the accident to my family in Japan," she says.

Oddly, and in an unexpected turn of events, the recovery period brought Hatsuko and Kalabula's hearts closer, to the point of them connecting emotionally. The strong feelings of love developed and evolved unconsciously. Hatsuko found Kalabula to be exceedingly caring, loving and kind. Among his several gestures of kindness, care and love, Kalabula prepared his aunty, an old lady who could not even speak English, to look after Hatsuko. This just melted Hatsuko's heart.

"I found his gesture very loving and kind," she reminisces.

As she made good progress in her recovery process, Hatsuko was highly impressed with the way Kalabula's family and friends helped in looking after her. She was very clear in her mind, as she put it, that "Zambians are good people."

Among them were prominent Ndola lawyer, Dr Julius Sakala's wife, and a very senior police officer's wife who visited her quite often.

"These are among the many that looked after me and gave me all the support, together with an Indian teacher who was as old as myself," she says.

Everyone who knew this 'couple' was by this time convinced beyond any reasonable doubt that Kalabula and Hatsuko were meant to be man and wife. So they started driving this agenda. But, by then, they were too late because the two hearts were already beating as one. Burning with the same desire, everything had fallen into place for Kalabula and Hatsuko. What remained was for Kalabula to formalise the marriage proposal. On her part, Hatsuko had written to Japan informing her family about the latest developments and her intention to remain in Zambia for at least the following two years.

Soon, Kalabula asked Hatsuko for her hand in marriage and she said, "Yes."

"He brought his mother with him, Elizabeth Kalabula from Mulobola Mission," Hatsuko remembers. "She asked me if I intended to go back to Japan. They all wanted me to remain in Zambia. She was unable to speak English but was a very nice lady. Mr Kalabula would interpret for me. She was totally illiterate, and when she watched television, she would ask why the people [on the screen] were moving and where they had disappeared to. We would just laugh about it."

Shortly thereafter, the two started making wedding arrangements.

"We just went to the civic centre at Ndola City Council to register the marriage as we could not go to church owing to my Buddhist status," she says. "He brought his Christian Bible and I brought my Buddhist one [the Tipitaka]. At the time, we lived in a two-bedroomed house in the school compound."

A little later, Kalabula took Hatsuko to his village in Mulobela in Kasama to meet the rest of his relatives and close family members. Upon arrival, they were welcomed with *Bemba* songs by the villagers who used buckets as improvised drums. Hatsuko still remembers how they slept in the sleeping bags they had brought with them from Ndola. Beds were available in the bedrooms but had no mattresses, so the sleeping bags were handy when it came to bedtime. The village houses did not have electricity.

"I enjoyed my experience in the village," she says. "Remember, I was tough-tested with my experiences in the Second World War, so that village experience was normal to me."

Kalabula and Hatsuko had two wedding ceremonies. The first one was in Ndola in 1978 and the second, a traditional Japanese ceremony in 1981, was in Okinawa, when it was Hatsuko's turn to introduce Kalabula to her family. Both ceremonies were prominently covered in the two countries' leading newspapers and the media in general.

The ceremony in Zambia was a simple tea party, held amidst Japanese floral arrangements. Hatsuko wore a Japanese kimono.

"We just called close relatives and friends for a simple ceremony," Kalabula would recall later in an interview before he died. "Money left over from the well-wishers we donated to the school for the blind."

The situation in Japan was quite different. Kalabula was pleasantly surprised by the welcome he received in Okinawa, right from the airport where a television crew was waiting to film the arrival of the couple.

"It was amazing," he recalled. "It was amazing to see the number of her relatives who came to the airport to welcome us. There were even television cameras. Her family members – close and distant – all came to the airport. They all had something to offer me. One offered a car for our use while we were in Okinawa. Another offered a deep freezer full of food for us to eat whilst there; and yet another one offered us a flat for lodging.

"There were so many people offering this and that. I was received very well, just like a leader from an African country. In fact, I was the first African that time to set foot on Okinawa Island. Of course, there were black Americans by virtue of the war that they had fought, but I think I was the first black civilian there."

Because of the incident that had brought them closer – the road traffic accident while travelling to Kawambwa – Hatsuko still jokes that she and Kalabula were "married by accident."

"That accident reinforced our feelings for each other and brought us closer together," Kalabula said. "She always referred to this incident, saying that we were married by accident because we became [emotionally] closer after the accident."

Being an interracial marriage, there were many challenges anticipated in the union. Hatsuko had to cope with the Zambian way of life. That notwithstanding, the couple navigated their respective cultural differences very well.

"I blended in very easily because of my experience with the Second World War," Hatsuko brags. "It was easy for me to survive in any situation. I was even able to queue up for cooking oil and sugar during the commodity shortages in the UNIP days and endure the *mishanga* boys [street boys selling cigarettes]. I integrated into Zambian society very well."

As is often said, the quickest way to learn a different culture is first to learn the language of that culture. In due course, Hatsuko learnt some basic Bemba words to help her communicate with the local people who could not speak English. And, as a phonetician, Hatsuko did not experience a lot of problems in pronouncing some Bemba words.

Kalabula explained that from the outset, Hatsuko and he resolved to establish their 'own culture' in a bid to escape possible misunderstandings due to their racial and cultural differences.

"From the beginning, I told myself that we were going to make our own culture, looking at her culture and my culture and then meet half way," he said. "But I think she has taken much more of the Bemba culture than I have of her culture. Whenever we have wedding ceremonies or funerals, she mixes with people very easily. She even attends kitchen parties. People at these parties are amazed because my wife is more Zambian than most young Zambians."

For Hatsuko, people everywhere are all the same. No wonder she had difficulties stating her race when she was asked for it in her visa application back in 1977.

"When you talk about culture, I find that as a people we are all the same, originally," she says. "Where I was born and brought up, on a small island in Japan, it was very similar to Africa or Zambia, to some Bemba traditions and customs. Humanity is there also."

But what are the similarities between the Zambian culture and that of Japan in Okinawa?

"How to live together, how to respect and be nice to other people," Hatsuko says. "We also lived in small, warm communities."

As if to apply the Zambian tradition, if not just implementing the Bible requirement for wives to have 'deep respect' for their husbands, Hatsuko addressed Kalabula as *batata* [my father], which was a bit awkward as she was 13 years his senior.

"I think it is an intimate expression, isn't it?" says Hatsuko. "I was being respectful to my husband. Could I have called him sweetheart? In Japan, no! So I thought *batata* is a good word to pick to show respect to my husband. I didn't want to call him darling, sweetheart or by his first name as Mwamba. I always called him *batata* as a sign of respect. Of course things have changed now with the young married couples. But in the 70s and 80s, I know that most Zambian men expected a lot of respect from wives in that way. It was most difficult to say my husband or address him by his first name."

Hatsuko and Kalabula were married for 31 years, until Kalabula died. Yet Hatsuko says marriage was never an easy undertaking but called for endurance, perseverance and tolerance.

"Marriage is tough everywhere. There are many potholes just like there are many smooth ways," she says. "If I were to tell you what my mother taught me before I came here, it would be a long story. But briefly, we are taught how to conduct ourselves in a marriage; whether there is rain, snow or sunshine; you have to survive, stick by your husband no matter how poor he is or how rich we are, we have to respect each other and make a proper home. Sometimes there is so much outside influence in a marriage, it's everywhere. It is all up to individuals living together."

But how has life been for Hatsuko, without her husband?

"As a Buddhist, I am ready to accept any sweet things or bad things," says Hatsuko. "I am comfortable because from the beginning, I was brought up to be self-reliant. I have a house in Japan just like I do in Zambia. So every year I visit Japan, but I spend three quarters of the year in Zambia because I start to miss Zambia the moment I arrive in Japan. So, in a year, the longest I would stay in Japan is three months, just to see my family and extended family members."

Hatsuko and Kalabula did not have any biological children, but they legally adopted several whom they looked after and educated. These are now living independent lives both in Zambia and abroad. But there is one, named Ipe, who still lives with Hatsuko, though in a separate house in her yard. He was adopted in the mid-1980s when he was about four months old.

Hatsuko named him Ipe and fondly calls him 'my Ipe'. She says, "Ipe means *peace* in Japanese and I called him Ipe because I wanted everyone to love him."

*** *** ***

SCHOOL OF EDUCATION

CHAPTER SIX

Multiple Blessings

✳✳✳

KALABULA and Hatsuko's marriage brought them multiple blessings. Both of them were passionate about education. Despite his humble beginnings and family financial difficulties resulting in his failure to complete Grade 12, Kalabula was determined to upgrade himself academically in later years.

After returning from Scotland and later obtaining six O'levels, Kalabula enrolled for a Bachelor's Degree in Education at the University of Zambia, which he did via 'correspondence' or distance learning.

TOP: Hatsuko, seated third from left in the second row with her brother, Chusei, on her right and his wife, Hiroko, on her left. They are surrounded by Chusei's four children – Yukie, Chieno, Yashushi and Junji – and their spouses and children. This photo was taken during Hatsuko's annual visit to Japan in 2012/13.

MIDDLE: (left) Hatsuko with Kalabula at his graduation with a master's degree at Birmingham University, USA, in the early 1990s; (right, above) another annual visit to Okinawa Island: Hatsuko, in the middle with her brother Chusei on the left, his wife Hiroko on the right.; behind is Hatsuko's niece, Chieno; (right, below) Hatsuko shaking hands with the great grandson of the Scottish explorer, Dr David Livingstone, when he paid a courtesy call on Dr Kenneth Kaunda at his office in Lusaka. Looking on are Dr Kaunda and Dr Kalabula. This was in the early 2000s.

BOTTOM: (left) Hatsuko, at her graduation with a master's degree in English and Literature at the University of Zambia, 2008; (right) with her fellow classmates in the Masters programme, 2007.

His wife was a source of both moral and financial support. She wanted him to obtain the highest university qualification, which he did – much to her delight.

In 1981, Kalabula left the school for the blind – which is now called Ndola Lions School for the Visually Impaired – to take up a higher position at the Ministry of Education headquarters in Lusaka as Senior Inspector of Schools for the blind. He was also tasked with establishing the Department of Special Education in the ministry.

"I encouraged him to go for further studies and study for a degree in special education since at that time we didn't have people with this qualification," says Hatsuko. "He was very key to special education and I encouraged him to interest as many people as possible so he could have a good successor."

As Kalabula worked in this position, he was also studying with the university via distance learning until in 1987 when he moved to campus on a full time basis. This was a year before completing his programme in 1988.

Hatsuko was delighted by Kalabula's achievement and encouraged him to further his studies immediately. Kalabula did just that, enrolling for a Master's programme at Birmingham University in the United States of America.

In 1992, Kalabula returned to Zambia as Dr Kalabula, having successfully completed his PhD programme. He continued working for the Ministry of Education until 1994 when he decided to go on early retirement in order to fulfill Hatsuko's condition for her sponsoring his PhD programme. The condition was for Dr Kalabula to join UNZA and help to establish a degree programme in special education in order to have more Zambians trained in special education.

"In 1994, I decided to take early retirement to join the University of Zambia and help to establish a degree programme for young people who are interested in teaching children with special needs," Dr Kalabula said, in an interview in 2007. "So, in 1996, we had the first intake. So far we have had five streams of students graduating from the programme. And I am very happy to say that 53 of the students that have graduated from the programme have been given responsible positions in the education system as district education [board] secretaries, district education officers and district education standards officers.

"Then we proceeded to postgraduate activities in our department at the university and we produced about 20 or so students, six of whom have been deployed in the department as lecturers after obtaining their degrees. Now we are extending to PhD studies. I think we have six young people on this programme."

Until February 2007, Dr Kalabula served as Head of the Special Education Department at UNZA. Thereafter, he concentrated his efforts on research, apart from supervising master and PhD students.

"I am also concentrating on publishing so that I can make a small contribution to the education of children with special needs," he said.

By the time he died in early 2008, Dr Kalabula's two books in standards evaluation were ready for publication. This is his rich legacy in the area of special education in Zambia, achieved with the kind and generous support from his loving and endearing wife, Hatsuko.

So, what inspired Dr Kalabula's love for special education?

"When I look at children with special needs, I find that they have equal rights," he explained. "If properly supported, they can gain their personal dignity and also contribute to their families, personal and national development. I have seen many examples of people, including many that I have taught who are disabled and have broken out of that cycle and now lead very respectable lives. I think that every human being has the potential to overcome whatever problem they have. In fact, the blind call me 'cousin of the blind' because I never consider them blind. I consider them just like any other person. If they bump into me, I jokingly ask them why they don't look where they are going."

For Hatsuko, Dr Kalabula's achievements in the area of special education in Zambia were a great honour and inspired her to remain in Zambia. Her efforts in encouraging and supporting her husband to pursue further education paid off, just as she had envisioned.

"This is our humble contribution," she says. "I am very happy that I encouraged him to go for his masters. After that, I also encouraged him to go for his PhD. I helped to sponsor him for three years. He had such a good brain. But I gave him a condition: when he gets his PhD, he must establish a degree course in special education at UNZA. He promised to do just that and he did just that. He produced a lot of BA (bachelor) and MA (master) students in special education at UNZA after he had helped to establish the School of Special Education."

As all this was happening, Hatsuko also revived her dream to study for a master's degree in literature and African studies. So she enrolled at UNZA and graduated in 2008. Initially, she had planned to obtain this qualification from Manchester University after graduating from the Moray House School of Education in Scotland in 1977. Hatsuko, however, abandoned the plan following her visit to Zambia the same year, and decided never to return to Manchester.

But one of the greatest achievements for the couple was the love that they built over the years, which was well-recognised.

On her birthday in December 2006, Dr Kalabula put an advert in one of the national newspapers to appreciate Hatsuko for everything she had done for him, his family and country. The message read:

Happy Birthday Darling Wife. Twenty-nine years ago, you left a very peaceful, prosperous and cozy Okinawa and brought your love to Zambia. Not only did you confine yourself to loving me, but you profoundly put your full heart into my family, my country, my country's people as the First Republican President of Zambia, His Excellency Dr Kenneth David Kaunda noted and I quote:

'Mrs Kalabula ... How much we must thank God our Creator to have provided for us a loving, hardworking and truly creative sister like you! Our beloved brother Kalabula must have been born a blessed one *to have such a wonderful wife – loving and caring for us all in Zambia.*

… I am personally very proud of you. Please know that you are profoundly appreciated and loved.

Hatsuko had met President Kenneth Kaunda (known colloquially as KK) for the first time in 1979, and they would become well acquainted over the years. In fact, Dr Kaunda referred to Hatsuko as 'my sister'.

Their first meeting happened when Hatsuko had led a small team from her school to exhibit at the Zambia International Trade Fair in Ndola. When President Kaunda neared the stand where the school was exhibiting, Hatsuko told the blind pupils to sing and beat their drums even more loudly.

"Then he came to our stand," she recalls. "I was so overwhelmed with happiness as though I was meeting my father. I was wearing a Japanese kimono. He was so impressed that I could take blind children on a public outing. In that era, most Zambian parents would hide their blind and handicapped children from the public. They wouldn't even allow them to attend school. So we tried to break that attitude. We composed a song for the blind children to sing, encouraging parents to expose such children to the public and school so they could be educated. That's the song KK listened to when he visited our stand. He was so impressed and gave me a lot of encouragement."

That was the beginning of Hatsuko's long friendship with Dr Kaunda.

"I liked KK because of his humanism philosophy," says Hatsuko.

Losing Batata

In 2008, tragedy struck the couple when Dr Kalabula died. Hatsuko's heart was shattered by the death of her *batata*.

It was in January, the peak of the rainy season, when Dr Kalabula travelled to Kabwe, in Central Province, for a workshop. He had been booked in at a government lodge.

According to Hatsuko, one night, Dr Kalabula went to sleep in his room and never woke up. The following day, some workers at the lodge became concerned after noticing that their guest had not come out of his room for breakfast that morning.

Later in the afternoon, when it became apparent something was amiss, the workers called the police, who forced open the door to his room.

Dr Kalabula lay lifeless in bed. A streak of dry blood ran from his nose. Police phoned Hatsuko, who was at home preparing for prayers that day, and informed her about her husband.

She travelled to Kabwe to bring back the body of her dead husband, and prepare it for burial. Because Dr Kalabula had converted to Buddhism, it meant his body had to be cremated as per custom.

Hatsuko says there was no objection from Dr Kalabula's family to have his body cremated. But back then, there was no proper crematorium in Lusaka.

"They just piled up some logs and put his body on top; it was horrible," says Hatsuko.

After the cremation, Hatsuko gathered the ash and some bones that had survived the fire and put them in an earthen pot she had bought on one of her trips to Kasama. That pot is stored in some place within the compound where she now lives.

After living inseparably for 31 years, Hatsuko had to learn how to live without her *batata*. But as a Second World War survivor, Hatsuko remained strong and promised to continue living in Zambia until her death.

She sold the family house in Kalundu suburb and relocated to a 25-acre plot she had acquired in 1988. It is located in Munali on the Great East Road in Lusaka. It stands on an undulating piece of land, opposite the Levy Mwanawasa University Teaching Hospital, on plot number 12905. And in one corner of the plot, surrounded by both indigenous and exotic trees, stands Hatsuko's small but beautiful cottage.

To most Zambians, the place is well-known for the Soka Gakkai International (SGI) Centre, which stands on the same plot.

SGI is an international Buddhist organisation which Hatsuko and Dr Kalabula helped to establish in Zambia to promote and espouse the principles and beliefs of Buddhism. This was done with the help from the SGI headquarters in Japan. In fact, Dr Kalabula served as director general of the organisation. The centre in Lusaka, SGI Zambia, was also meant to cater for the entire southern Africa.

SGI was founded in Japan after the Second World War in 1947 by a famous Japanese philosopher, author, poet, educator, peacebuilder and Buddhist named Daisaku Ikeda. He was only 19 when he established the organisation.

Ikeda embarked on a peace mission after seeing the destruction of human life in Japan's cities of Hiroshima and Nagasaki during the World War. The two cities suffered immense destruction after atomic bombs were dropped on them by the United States of America between August 6 and 9 in 1945, which ended the Second World War.

It is estimated that 355,000 people – mostly civilians – perished in the destruction. It was the first time that nuclear weapons were used in conflict and resulted in international treaties limiting their use because of the huge scale of devastation seen in the two cities.

Ikeda's four older brothers had been drafted into military service and the eldest was killed in action.

Ikeda had seen enough human suffering resulting from the war, and decided to pursue peace. It is said that one day, he walked into a meeting and witnessed Josei Toda – who later became his mentor – talking about peace and the need to respect each individual's human life. Ikeda became deeply interested and decided to devote himself to being a peace ambassador and to spread the message of peace across the world.

After the death of Toda, Ikeda became SGI president and made a trip to America, and he would later talk to world leaders about the need for peace.

For close on five decades, Ikeda – who became the first president of SGI International in 1975 – has spoken to many powerful and influential institutions worldwide, and he has given speeches and lectures at more than 30 universities, including Harvard.

By 2007, he had received numerous honorary degrees from various universities and several citizenships across the world. SGI International, which has over 12 million members, operates in a good number of countries in the world. Zambia's centre serves as the hub for the southern Africa region. It came as a donation from Ikeda, who was motivated by the small building that Hatsuko and her husband had put together. Daisaku Ikeda died in November 2023.

"I applied for this land from the council because I wanted to build a school," narrates Hatsuko. "That time I didn't have SGI in mind. I was just thinking about my own school and women's college, a youth centre and sports field. I wanted to establish a school from pre-primary to primary. That's a very important age to instil any basic knowledge and morals. But instead I started the women's academy in Chilenje township in 1994. It helped to empower women by teaching them how to do tie-and-dye and sew school uniforms, among other skills. Those who graduated with flying colours were rewarded with sewing machines. I couldn't construct the school as envisaged because I started concentrating on Buddhism through SGI. But now I regret not having done so."

In 2020, Hatsuko was awarded a medal, the Order of the Rising Sun, Gold and Silver Rays, by the Japanese Emperor, for her distinguished service in deepening the mutual relationship and friendship between Zambia and Japan. This medal is awarded to people who have rendered distinguished service to the Japanese government in various fields, including contributions to the stability and development of the international community.

The then Japanese ambassador to Zambia, Mr Mizuuchi Ryuta, presented the award to Hatsuko at his residence in Lusaka on January 16, 2020, on behalf of the emperor. The ceremony was attended by Hatsuko's longtime friends, who included Zambia's former vice-president Enoch Kavindele, former health minister Prof. Nkandu

Luo, former UNZA vice-chancellor Prof. Robert Serpel and Prof. Lloyd Mulenga, director for Infectious Diseases at the Ministry of Health in Zambia.

But it is not only people with titles and high status that Hatsuko made friends with. Over the years, she has established friendships with Zambians from different backgrounds, including people from the townships, whom she says have a lot of human interest stories to tell. These include some of the men and women who work for her.

"If you want to know the political temperature in the country, these are the people to listen to and listen attentively," says Hatsuko.

Hatsuko also founded and chaired the Zambia–Japan Friendship Association in 1988 as a way of entrenching the collaboration and friendship between the two countries. Through the association, a scholarship was introduced in the School of Veterinary Medicine at the University of Zambia. The association also promoted youth sports exchange programme that were aimed at promoting the cultures of the two countries.

This was in addition to the material and financial assistance Hatsuko continued to procure specifically for the Ndola Lions School for the Visually Impaired and the Ministry of Education in general. She also acquired some vehicles, including a 34-seater Rosa minibus.

Hatsuko also sponsored a number of students at the University of Zambia, particularly those who studied medicine. That was largely because of her experience in 1978 when she was involved in a road accident and ended up in Ndola Central Hospital where she only found doctors who were mostly from Asian countries. There was no indigenous doctor working at the hospital, which is why she resolved deliberately to support the education of student doctors at the University of Zambia.

A number of students who were sponsored by Hatsuko later held influential positions in various health facilities, government, and the University of Zambia. One such student was Dr Kennedy Malama, who once served as Permanent Secretary in the Ministry of Health.

"I was sponsoring two boys when he [Dr Malama] came in," Hatsuko recollects. "That time there was free education. Students were being sponsored 100 percent by KK's government, but it was not enough, according to me. So I supplemented them with 50 percent of whatever the government paid them. I sponsored medical students and those who studied chemistry."

Hatsuko chose to withhold the names of the many students she sponsored, only singling out Dr Malama because of his honesty and transparency when it came to the money she donated to him.

Of course she never demanded or expected receipts from the sponsored students to acquit themselves as she was certain they would utilise the money for its intended purposes.

"Malama had heard about this and he approached me for similar help," she recalls. "He came from Northern Province. So I always subsidised him with 700 Kwacha and he always brought receipts to account for his expenditure. But the other two never did. Up to now, Dr Malama is in touch with me."

Despite the long passage of time, the current management at the Ndola Lions School for the Visually Impaired still remembers and honours Hatsuko's various contributions to the school, which has grown and flourished over the years with her support. As at February 2023, the school had over 120 learners from Grade One to Twelve.

"Initially, the school only went up Grade Five, from Grade One," the school's headmaster, Mr Alick Chewe, said. "The majority of teachers now are former pupils from the school. Out of our current complement of 22 teachers, 4 are sighted and 18 are visually impaired. Of those 18, about 12 passed through here, they are our former pupils."

According to Mr Chewe, the school was now deliberately encouraging its learners to diversify in their career choices.

"We are now encouraging them to pursue careers other than teaching," he said. "In 2022, we had a boy who had seven points in Grade 12. He said he wanted to be a lawyer and I encouraged him to

HATSUKO was in January 2020 honoured with the medal – the Order of the Rising Sun, Gold and Silver Rays – by the Japanese emperor for her distinguished service in deepening the mutual relationship between Zambia and Japan. Here, Hatsuko showing off the medal after receiving the award from the then Japanese ambassador to Zambia, Mr Mizuuchi Ryuta (standing behind Hatsuko, on behalf of the emperor) at his residence in Lusaka. With her, among others, are Zambia's former Vice-President Enoch Kavindele, former Health Minister Professor Nkandu Luo, former Inspector General of Police Kakoma Kanganja, former UNZA Vice-Chancellor Professor Robert Serpel, Dr Kenneth Kaunda's son – Dr Waza Kaunda – and one of Zambia's most renowned medical practitioners, Prof. Lloyd Mulenga.

go for it so we can have a visually impaired lawyer … Technology has assisted our friends in the advanced countries.

You can imagine [our learner obtaining] seven points with the limitations of study materials because most of the books are in print and not braille. We are crying for a braille machine to transcribe our books from print to braille. This will help in pushing up the quality of the education we are giving to these visually impaired learners. For now, most of them need to have someone reading aloud to them."

Mr Manasseh Mulenga, a former pupil and now a teacher at the school, says he enrolled in the school in 1986 and completed his education at Munali School in Lusaka. He is now a teacher of English.

"I learnt about Mrs Takara-Kalabula in 1986 when I came here because of her contributions to the school," says Manasseh.

****

Photograph: Amos Malupenga

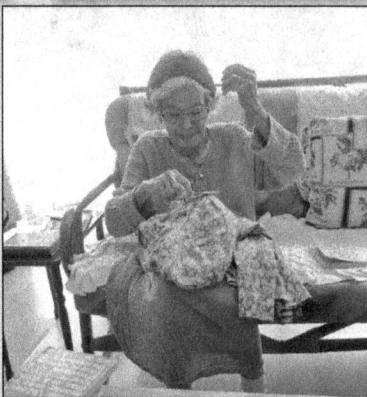

Photograph: Amos Malupenga

Photograph: Ipe Kalabula

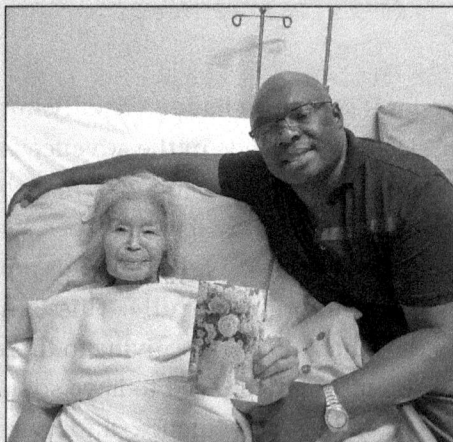

TOP: (left) Hatsuko with two of her brother's grandsons during one of her visits to Japan; (right) Hatsuko, cleaning plates in her cottage's kitchen in Lusaka as part of her chores routine, 2023.

MIDDLE: (left) Hatsuko, visiting Dr Kenneth Kaunda at his residence; (right) Hatsuko, in February 2023, mending the dress she bought at London's Harrods departmental shop in 1975.

BOTTOM: (left) Hatsuko, with her brother's other grandson in Japan; (right) the author visiting Hatsuko at University Teaching Hospital in Lusaka where she was admitted in April 2023.

Longevity

✳✳✳

Aaccording to the Oxford English Dictionary, longevity simply means long life; living a long and healthy life. Longevity is how long a person is going to live, and how healthy his or her later life will be. In other words, longevity describes the condition of a person living beyond the average life expectancy.

According to the World Health Organisation, Zambia's life expectancy "at birth has improved by 18 years from 44.5 years in 2000 to 62.5 years in 2019." And Macrotrends reports that as at 2023, Zambia's life expectancy stood at 64.70 years, reflecting a continuous improvement.

For Japan, life expectancy in 2023 was estimated at 85.03 years, a 0.14 percent increase from 2022 at 84.91 years.

And, according to the *World Population Review*, in 2023, Monaco – the second-smallest country in the world after the Vatican City, with an area of 2.02 square kilometres and an estimated population of 40,000 people (2023) – had the highest life expectancy in the world standing at an average of 87 years.

By comparison, Russia is the biggest country in the world with a total area of 17,098,246 square kilometres and a life expectancy of 73.3 years as at the first quarter of 2023.

At the time of my conversation with Hatsuko in January 2023, she had turned 89 years old just a month earlier, but she was still able to read – even text in a small font size – without the aid of glasses. In fact, some people mistake her clear sunglasses for spectacles or reading glasses.

Hatsuko was also able to carry out some chores despite having a housemaid. Throughout her life, Hatsuko has enjoyed good health and, except after the car accident she was involved in back in 1978, was never admitted to hospital until January 2023 when she ate ice-cream which upset her stomach and had to be kept in hospital overnight for observation.

Her next hospital admission was three months later when she tripped and fell at home, dislocating her hip. Despite her advanced age, Hatsuko recovered from that hip dislocation amazingly quickly. She was hospitalised for a few months, initially in Zambia and later in Japan where she sought further treatment.

A few surgical procedures were performed on her. As a result, she was confined to a wheelchair as part of the recovery process. Hatsuko was so uncomfortable in this chair because she was used to walking about. This discomfort, perhaps, quickened her recovery process because she soon graduated to a walker and later a walking stick before she walked by herself. Of course, from time to time, she sparingly uses the wheelchair to consolidate the recovery.

When I reconnected with her in January 2023 after 16 years, I was astounded by her excellent elephant's memory despite being 89 years old. She recollected, with such clarity, everything we had shared in those two years before we lost touch in 2008. I was even more astounded when I started recording her life history. She demonstrated a marvellous ability to recall events in her life with precision.

This is a very rare ability which very few people possess, according to research. Scientists, particularly neurobiologists, call this condition *hyperthymesia,* which is also known as Highly Superior Autobiographical Memory (HSAM).

This is the uncommon ability that allows a person to recall, spontaneously, almost every event in their life with great detail and accuracy. So far, scientists have established – through research – that this ability is limited to 'autobiographical memories', that is to say people can only recall, with precision, information about themselves and their past personal experiences.

This, therefore, may explain why a person's 'good memory' is different from HSAM. A 'good memory' is the mental capacity to retain and revive events, facts, experiences and impressions, among others, using mnemonic devices, while people with HSAM do not use mnemonic devices.

A mnemonic device, or memory device, is "any learning technique that aids information retention or retrieval (remembering) in the human memory for better understanding." Songs and rhymes can be used as very good examples of effective mnemonic devices. Recall how, as young children, at least during my time, we were taught to remember the entire alphabet of 26 letters (from A–Z) in a row by reciting a simple rhyming tune?

Anyhow, pardon my brief digression. Hatsuko's admirable HSAM sparked it.

No wonder, though, that neurobiologists are currently studying this phenomenon to understand how a human brain processes such memories. I am afraid they will never find a satisfactory answer to this most perplexing and awe-inspiring issue which only goes to demonstrate the unimaginable sophistication of the Grand Creator who magnificently created all things – Jehovah God. His glorious magnificence is beyond human understanding.

Back to the subject of longevity. Asians – and the Japanese in particular – are known to have long lifespans. Research has shown that over two million people in Japan are older than 90 years and more than 70,000 are 100 years old or more.

Some people believe this has to do with their genes. Contrary to this popular belief, Hatsuko says longevity among the Japanese is not due to their genes, but rather their lifestyle and diet. This is also confirmed by research.

Various scientific studies have concluded that the Japanese consume lots of fresh vegetables as well as seasonal and unprocessed foods, resulting an obesity rate of about 3.6 percent, the lowest in the world. They also love seafood, with Japan ranking among the top six nations for fish consumption. Naturally, fish has lower cholesterol and saturated fat compared to red meat, thereby reducing the risk of death by heart disease by 36 percent.

The Japanese also eat a lot of soy and seaweed, with an estimated 100,000 tonnes of seaweed consumed in Japan every year. Seaweed contains natural iodine which is useful for regulating thyroid and contains somewhere between two and nine grams of proteins per cup.

Besides watching their diets, the Japanese practise portion control, eating much smaller food portions per meal than other countries. This habit is good for controlling body weight and digestion.

Another reason why the Japanese live longer than most other peoples, scientists say, is because they drink plenty of tea which contains far more antioxidants than coffee, boosting their immune systems and helping to prevent cancer and excess cholesterol.

In addition, the Japanese stay active, often walking or biking to work. The older people in Japan continue to engage in physical activity for as long as they can. Furthermore, about 85 percent of Japanese people end their day in a hot bath, which allows for detoxification through sweating, reduces inflammation, relieves stress, improves blood circulation and boosts their immune system.

Japan also has one of the most efficient healthcare systems in the world.

The elderly, in Japan, are considered living treasures, and are afforded the utmost respect, helping them to enjoy their time and live longer lives.

And so at 90, Hatsuko is still able to carry out a lot of activities – albeit on a lighter scale. Activity is the key word to explaining her longevity. She is very active, engaging daily in some light house chores and exercising by walking short distances within her property.

"I attribute my long, healthy life to my active use of my two legs," she says. "I am not lazy, because in Japan we are able to count, on a daily basis, how many steps one has walked. That's key to a healthy life. Being overly dependent on a car to get you from place to place shortens your life. Physical exercise is important, especially the exercise of walking on two legs every day. As you exercise by walking, it is also important that you greet and chat with those you meet on the way. This is very important for your health."

Hatsuko further advises: "Walking is healthier than using the minibus or a car. Japanese like exercising a lot. They park their cars and walk. Don't be too idle. Early in the morning, I walk up to the roadside. I also walk about in the yard. I am happy also that in my yard, we have a lot of trees which provide good oxygen." And in jest, Hatsuko says her numerous trees help in 'providing' oxygen to the Levy Mwanawasa Hospital which is opposite her property.

When it comes to food, Hatsuko enjoys Zambia's cuisine as much as she does the Japanese one.

"Nshima [pap, a thick maize-meal porridge] and kapenta is my favourite meal," she says. "Kapenta is in two types, *Mpulungu* and *Siavonga*. Mpulungu kapenta is harder but tastier. Generally, I eat more of vegetables than anything else. I enjoy pumpkin leaves mixed with groundnut powder. I also enjoy sweet potatoes *yakusashila* [in thick groundnut soup]."

Hatsuko says the Japanese culture of eating smallish portions of food at meals contributes to their much talked about longevity.

"We are told that even when you have a lot of food, the stomach must only be filled between 70 and 80 percent, not in full," she says. "No matter how delicious the meal is, the stomach must only be filled up to 80 percent maximum during day-time meals and 70 percent in the evening. This is what we learn from family education and it contributes to longevity. You have to train your mind to always stop eating at that point when you start to enjoy the meal the most."

The other key contributing factor to longevity is self-discipline and positivity, according to Hatsuko.

"If you bring negativity in your life, this negativity will crush you," she says. "So smile and have positive thoughts and things will move in such a way. I also read a lot. This is good for my active mind."

Hatsuko's typical day starts at 5am when she takes off her nightclothes and puts on a smart dress and makes a cup of coffee or tea for herself.

"I have to dress smart because after coffee or tea, I start my prayers to unlock my own potential for what I can achieve that day and fulfil my dream," she says. "That's why I cannot pray whilst dressed in my pajamas."

Like Hatsuko, I also enjoy praying and reading my favourite book – the Holy Bible – which states that man's lifespan is at least 70 years or, at most, 80.

Life beyond 70 or 80 years will be full of "trouble" and "sorrow"; it will be a struggle. This is how it's recorded in Psalm 90:10: "The span of our life is 70 years, or 80 if one is especially strong. But they are filled with trouble and sorrow; they quickly pass by, and away we fly."

Whatever the case, "life" – going by the widely used cliché – "is as short as a whisper" and our years come to an end like a whisper. James 4:13–15, advises: "Come, now, you who say: 'Today or tomorrow we will travel to this city and we will spend a year there, and we will do business and make some profit,' whereas you do not know what your life will be like tomorrow. For you are a mist that appears for a little while and then disappears. Instead, you should say: 'If Jehovah wills, we will live and do this or that'."

What is the meaning of this statement? In my opinion, as human beings, we are not in control or in charge of our lives or affairs,

HATSUKO in the front row with her brother Chusei and his wife Hiroko, posing with their children and the children's spouses, Okinawa, 2019.

regardless of what we do to enhance our health in order to increase our lifespans. We can make plans for tomorrow or next year but fail to achieve them because life may be cut short at any time. Our lives may be short or long. We can check our lifestyles and do everything it takes to achieve longevity and yet still die 'prematurely'. In fact, there is no 'mature' death because human beings were created to live eternally, forever. That is all the more reason we do everything or anything in our power to prolong our lives. And no wonder every death is described as being 'untimely'.

Indeed, life is like a 'mist'. It appears for a little while and then disappears. Therefore, we should praise and thank Jehovah God our Creator daily for the gift of life and supplicate that He continues to bless us with good health for each day we experience. It does not belong to us, even to direct our own steps.

*** *** ***

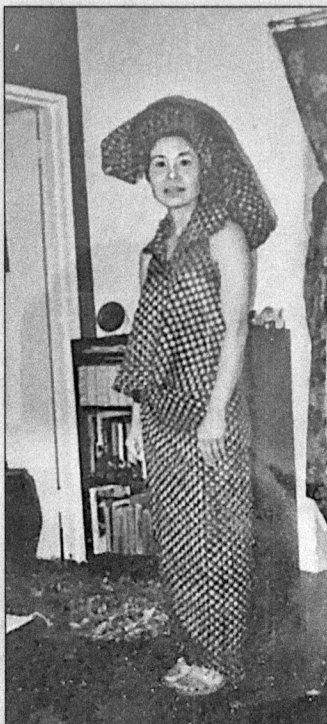

Photograph: Amos Malupenga

Photograph: Amos Malupenga

TOP: (left) Hatsuko and Dr Kalabula outside the SGI Centre in Lusaka, 2007; (right) Hatsuko, attired in a Chitenge material outfit with a matching headdress, which were tailor-made for her as a special gift from Dr Kalabula when she first came to Zambia in 1977.

BOTTOM: (left) Hatsuko, displaying the two differently designed urns. According to her wish, these are the containers that she bought to contain the remains of her body after cremation; July 21, 2023; (right) a close-up of one of the urns; July 21, 2023.

Cremation and the Urn

✳✳✳

From time immemorial, death has remained a mystery that has continued to puzzle humanity. People from different cultural, racial and other backgrounds treat the subject of death in different ways.

For many, discussing death or planning for it is taboo before it occurs. And when it does, only adults discuss it to make funeral arrangements and to decide what to do with the deceased's possessions. No wonder for many Zambians, it is still considered an alien practice to draw up a will and final testament, the legal document that communicates a person's final wishes pertaining to their assets. It provides specific instructions about what to do with their possessions, including liabilities. It indicates whether the deceased leaves the assets to another person such as a spouse and children, a group, or wishes to donate them to charity.

In recent years, however, the trend is changing in the Zambian context. More and more Zambians are embracing this concept, especially after observing or witnessing very undesirable scenes of property grabbing where some family members have been deprived or literally robbed of valuable assets following the death of breadwinners. Most orphaned children and widows have been deprived of properties, including real estate.

As many try to secure assets for their families and loved ones through wills and testaments, some have gone as far as stating how they wish to be mourned and buried once they die. A few have even opted for cremation, something still strange in Zambia.

Nevertheless, for Hatsuko, a practising Buddhist, discussing her own death and preparing for its aftermath, comes almost naturally. She says Buddhists are encouraged to prepare for all eventualities.

Having turned 90 in December 2023, Hatsuko feels her death can occur at any time and so she is ready for it. She spent some time discussing with me how 'quiet and calm' she wanted her funeral to be. She has even bought a set of two urns to contain her remains after the cremation of her body.

In the Zambian context, this is like someone buying a casket or coffin which they wish to be buried in. Not very long ago, this practice was almost alien in Zambia, although a few non-indigenous Zambians have done this in the recent past. Not anymore. Now some indigenous Zambians have secured or purchased family plots for graves either in the public cemeteries or private properties. This practice never existed before.

As an aside, I know of one non-indigenous Zambian who actually did not buy his own casket, but instead made it over a period of years. A rather bizarre thing for one to do! He was buried in it at Lusaka's Memorial Park.

Hatsuko bought two urns because she wants her ashes to be shared between Zambia and Japan. She is a Japanese citizen but a Zambian resident. She prefers her ashes to be buried in Zambia but to have some available to be exported to Japan, should her relatives insist that her ashes be buried in Japan.

"When I die, my body should be wrapped in the *chitenge* dress which *batata* gifted me the first time I visited Zambia in 1977," she says. "This *chitenge* is so special to me and I have kept it all these years; a very fine *chitenge* outfit with a headdress; very beautiful. He asked a [young] lady to make this special *chitenge* outfit which I still keep. So, when I die, it is my wish to be wrapped in that *chitenge* before my body is cremated." The top part of the *chitenge* outfit (headdress and blouse) is in Lusaka while the bottom part (wrapper) is in Japan.

"I am 90, so I have prepared for everything, including my death and cremation. I have enjoyed living in Zambia since 1977. I was curious to know everything about Zambia, its people and culture. Zambians are very kind people."

Looking back at the genesis of her trip to Zambia, Hatsuko does not regret that what was meant to be a visit to Zambia ended in permanent residence.

"I am a Japanese citizen and a Zambian resident but my heart is in Zambia so I will be buried in Zambia," she says. "We believe in cremation, so I bought these urns in Okinawa to be used when I die. My ashes will be kept in one, in Zambia, but if my relatives want part of my remains, some can be put in the other urn and transported to Japan. I have to be ready so I don't give any difficulties to my family."

And, as if she were bidding farewell to Zambia and its friendly people, Hatsuko delightfully declared how she had enjoyed friendships with different Zambians over the years.

"I came alone but I made a lot of friends in Zambia," she says, holding the urn's lid in one hand and the container in the other. "Thank you very much you citizens of Zambia. Stay well and I end by offering you my favourite song in *Bemba* encouraging hard work." She then burst into singing this song in a melodious voice:

Bane mwebena Zambia	[*Fellow Zambians*]
Natubombe imilimo	[*Let's work*]
Pantu twalichulile]	[*Because we suffered*]
Lelo tuleiteka	[*Today we are governing ourselves*]
Ilyo bale tuteka	[*When they ruled us*]
Twali fye pamo ngabeni	[*We were like foreigners*]

Twalelala mumpanga.	[*We used to sleep in the bush*]
Lelo tuleiteka.	[*Today we are governing] ourselves*]
Iwe we mulumendo	[*You, young man*]
Nobe wemukashana	[*And you young woman*]
Ima ubombe namaka	[*Get up and work hard*]
Lelo tuleiteka	[*Today we are governing ourselves*]
Ici chalo tuleikalamo	[*This country we live in*]
Ni Lesa ewa tupele	[*It's God who gave it to us*]
Natutotele Kabumba	[*Let us thank the Creator*]
Lelo tuleiteka.	[*Today we are governing ourselves*]
Iwe wemunang'ani	[*You, the lazy one*]
Bula ulukasu lobe	[*Get your hoe*]
Ubombele bamwano	[*Work for your people*]
Lelo tuleiteka	[*Today we are governing ourselves*]

"This is my favourite song from 1977 up to now," says Hatsuko, of the song by one of Zambia's most celebrated and heroic musicians, the late Mpundu Mponde Mutale, who played an essential role during the freedom struggle, including through music. Most Zambians would remember his all-time great song titled, *"Africa, My Africa"*. The song sung by Hatsuko, titled, *"Lelo Tuleiteka"* is from that album.

"I also have another favourite *[Bemba]* song, talking about the importance of education," she said, in reference to another hit song by the late legend Emmanuel Mulemena. "Life continues and let's work together as Zambians. One Zambia, One Nation! *Natotela sana mwana wandi* [Thank you very much, my son]."

Hatsuko's visitors' book contains many messages left by people whom she touched with her humanity – her love and kindness.

Dr Chitalu Chilufya, minister of health at the time, visited Hatsuko on November 22, 2020 and left this message in her visitors' book:

An extraordinary life led. Contributed significantly to the development of the education of the disabled, particularly the blind; contributed to human capital and development in the health sector. Life inspired by God. Admirable legacy she has lived. A true living legend.

Another entry in Hatsuko's visitors' book is by Suresh Gupta – a prominent businessman – on December 12, 2020. He wrote:

> Known Mrs Kalabula for over 30 years. She is very kind-hearted with immense strength even at her age; strong presence of mind. She has contributed greatly to humanity and the Zambian community at large. She is an inspiration to all. I wish her good health, long life and best wishes always.

Mundia Mwitumwa, a renowned medical practitioner in Lusaka who visited on February 23, 2021, wrote:

> You are truly an angel sent from heaven. Thank you for your kindness and warmth. You are a great inspiration. May God continue to bless you and give you many more years to live.

Prof. Lloyd Mulenga, another renowned medical practitioner, visited Hatsuko in February 2021 and wrote:

> A brilliant and wonderful person. An educator, a bubbly individual committed to the social wellbeing of humanity. Her dedication to the preservation of culture is admirable. Her hospitality and openness ... in tough times is a rare quality. God bless you and grant you a long life.

And when I visited her on January 24, 2023, Hatsuko treated me to her old, cherished tradition of asking her visitors to leave a few words in her visitors' book. And so I penned my thoughts:

> It is so refreshing for me to link up with you after such a long time, almost 17 years. I am most delighted to find you in good health with your usual jovial disposition. May Jehovah God grant you more years on earth. Happy New Year [2023]. Sincerely, Amos Malupenga.

*** *** ***

EPILOGUE

Hatsuko's Humility

✳✳✳

HATSUKO'S desire was to have her life-story told in a simple way because she considers herself a simple human being. It is, therefore, my hope that I have told her story with the simplicity she desired, as she now looks forward to becoming a centenarian.

"When I turn 100 years, we will have a barbecue garden party," is Hatsuko's wish.

But of course life is like a mist, and only Jehovah our Creator knows our days on earth. Therefore, we must all learn to number our days, and appreciate the blessings that Jehovah brings in our lives, including the people He allows us to meet and learn from – people like Hatsuko.

She left her home country, Japan, still reeling from the horrors of the Second World War, to spread love and kindness among people that did not look like her or speak like her, loving them as her own kindred, including those that society looked down upon because of their physical condition.

Hatsuko's life-story has not been told in full, but I believe that her heart – her love and kindness – has been well captured between the covers of this book.

I have no doubt in my mind that Hatsuko's footprints will remain in the sand of her adopted country long after she is gone.

The lives she touched with her kindness, love and humility will never forget her amiable face.

Dictionaries generally define humility as a 'lowliness of mind'. Humility is the opposite of haughtiness; which is arrogance and pride. A humble person enjoys freedom from arrogance and pride because he or she considers others to be more important than him- or herself.

Pride and arrogance, which make one feel more superior to others, give birth to racism and many other social injustices, glaringly prevalent worldwide today.

This can only be overcome once people, as Martin Luther King Jr. said, stop judging each other by the colour of their skin, but by the content of their character.

That is what Hatsuko did. She broke many barriers in her life, not least the racial barrier, when she not only married an African man, but also assimilated his culture and embraced his people as her own.

She also broke the social barriers that put people in different classes based on economic status or level of education.

As Prof. Patrick Lumumba, the Kenyan legal luminary, once postulated about race: "There is only one race in the world, the human race. And we better learn that quickly. The faster we do so, the safer we are. So, first we must look at each other as human beings and we need each other. Once we recognise that, we must engage with each other from a position of mutual respect and mutual strength."

That's precisely what Hatsuko did. In fact, as you will recall, she was 'confused' when she was asked to state her 'race' when she applied for a visa at the Zambian High Commission in London in 1977. Her response was that she only knew of one race, the human race. This belief continued when she set foot in Zambia. Hatsuko did not discriminate on the basis of colour, ethnic group, cultural background or creed. She treated all human beings the same, and she still does.

Hatsuko also provides a great lesson about true love in the way she lived with her husband in a marriage spanning three decades. Although she came from a wealthy family, Hatsuko did not consider it degrading to marry someone from a poor background. Instead, she focused on the dream and vision that drove her future husband and made these her own by supporting him sacrificially to achieve his full potential; and he did, by obtaining a doctorate in his field of special education and being instrumental in promoting the education of children with special needs.

And Hatsuko showed her husband, who was 13 years her junior, deep respect, affectionately addressing him as *batata*. She had deliberately chosen to use *batata* in order to recognise her husband's headship in the family whilst willingly and lovingly displaying her submission to his role. Even in his death, she continues to refer to him as such.

Hatsuko lived her life selflessly, making huge sacrifices for others. Whether it was withdrawing from university in order to start work to look after her ailing mother and support her younger brother in university or volunteering as a staff member at a school for the visually-impaired, Hatsuko always exhibited a selfless spirit.

For this, Hatsuko is a true human being filled with humility.

****

HATSUKO, ever generous to her visitors. In case of the author, Amos Malupenga, she always has something to gift him, if not a meal or coffee, each time he visits her. Here, the author is captured appreciating Hatsuko after she gifted him a special whiskey glass made in Okinawa, Japan. This was during one of the author's visits in February 2023.